ALOE VERA FARMING

HOW TO START A PROFITABLE ALOE VERA FARM

BY Lucky James

Table of Contents

Chapter one: Introduction to Aloe Vera farming

Without been told Aloe Vera is known to be an important traditional medicine plant that belong to the family of Liliaceae. Today Aloe Vera is known by several names like Ghrit Kumari, Kunvar pathu and Indian Aloe. Aloe Vera plant is widely cultivated because of its wide adaptability and it use as a medicinal plant especially in dry areas. Aloe Vera is an indigenous plant to Africa and Mediterranean countries.

Furthermore, there are about 150 species in Aloe. Among this Aloe species, there is only one variety that has a legendary medical reputation dating back thousands of years, it is the Aloe Vera. The word Aloe is derived from the Arabic "alloeh" which means "bitter" because of bitter liquid found in the leaves. Aloe is a very good substitute to the synthetic ingredients now being used in cosmetic industry. One of the oldest plants ever known that is been use worldwide as a medicinal plant is Aloe Vera. This plant is a very powerful detoxifier, antiseptic and tonic for the nervous system. Aloe Vera plant also has immune-boosting and antiviral properties. Aloe Vera plants have a lot of health benefit. The following are some of the health benefit of Aloe Vera plant;

1. Aloe Vera plant contains healthful plant compounds.
2. Aloe Vera plants really contain antioxidant and antibacterial properties.
3. Aloe Vera plant can be use to accelerates the healing of burns.
4. Aloe Vera plant is use to reduces dental plaque.
5. Aloe Vera plant can really help to treat canker sores.

6. Aloe Vera plant can help to reduces constipation.
7. Aloe Vera plant can improve the skin and also prevent wrinkles.
8. Aloe Vera plant can help to Lower blood sugar levels.

There are a lot of health benefits of Aloe Vera plant.

Chapter two: Different types of Aloe Vera

There are different types of aloe Vera plant. The following are the different types of Aloe Vera plant;

1. The Aloe ciliaris species: This particular type is also known as climbing aloe. The Aloe ciliaris is thin and tough and grows incredibly fast. The Aloe ciliaris produces tubular flowers that are bright red-orange in color and it has a creamy-yellow tips. Below is the image.

2. The Aloe x principis species: This type of Aloe can grow up to 9 feet in height, it produces spikes in winter that are bright scarlet or orange in color and therefore it brightens up any Winter garden. This Aloe is a native of South Africa, The Aloe x principis is deer-resistant, very attractive to birds and bees. Below is the image.

3. The Arabian Aloe species (Aloe rubroviolacea): This particular type of Aloe can grow up to 3 feet high and 6 feet wide, this Aloe does best in soil that is well-drained and in bright full sun. Below is the image.

4. The Barbados Aloe species (Aloe barbadensis): The Barbados aloe really has a unique look. The leaves are facing upwards towards the sky. Below is the image.

5. The Cape Aloe species (Aloe ferox): The Cape Aloe (Aloe ferox) is a native to South Africa, The Cape Aloe consists of blue-green leaves that often have tinges of rose and they are up to 3 feet long. Below is the image.

6. The Coral Aloe species (Aloe striata): The Coral Aloe (Aloe striata) can grow up to 18 feet high and 18 feet in width. The Coral Aloe (Aloe striata) has flat, broad leaves that are pale grey-green in color but they turn pink in the sun and a more bluish color in the shade. Below is the image.

7. The Crosby's Prolific species : The Crosby's Prolific is a beautiful dwarf aloe. The Crosby's Prolific has a long green leaves that contain translucent teeth along its edges. The Crosby's Prolific can get up to 12 inches high and 15 inches wide, and it has fleshy leaves that get redder when it is sunny and hot, below is the image.

8. The Fan Aloe species (Aloe plicatilis): The Fan Aloe (Aloe plicatilis) consists of slender, long leaves that form a fan-like structure. The Fan Aloe (Aloe plicatilis) leaves are blue-grey in color and they have bright-orange

tips, and spikes of orange-red flowers. Below is the image.

9. The Golden Toothed Aloe species (Aloe nobilis): The Golden Toothed Aloe has triangle leaves that are bright-green in color and also include whitish teeth along the sides. The Golden Toothed Aloe leaves can turn an amazing orange color when they are in the full sun. Below is the image.

10.   The Mountain Aloe species (Aloe marlothii): The Mountain Aloe grows up to 10 feet high and is perfect for accents, borders, and containers. The Mountain Aloe flowers start out bright orange-red but later turn to yellow or bright-red. The Mountain Aloe is very attractive to birds and bees. Below is the image.

11.   The Red Aloe species (Aloe cameronii): The Red Aloe has colors that range from green to copper-red, with bright orange-red flowers appearing in early winter. The Red Aloe can grow up to 2 feet high and 4 feet in width. Below is the image.

Chapter three: How to plant Aloe Vera

The Soil and climate requirement

One thing about Aloe Vera plant is that they grow in hot humid and high rainfall conditions. Aloe Vera plant grows in all kind of soils but a well-drained soil with high organic matter, is most suitable. Aloe Vera plant grows well in bright sun light. If the environment is Shady it can results to disease infestation. Aloe Vera plant is highly sensitive to water stagnation. Make sure you select a well drain high land for cultivation. The Aloe Vera plant will do very well when supplied with an excess of 50 cm of rain annually. Try as much as possible to maintain the soil nitrogen at 0.40%–0.50%.

The Land Preparation for the Aloe Vera plant

Try as much as possible to carry out 2-3 ploughing and laddering to make the soil weed free and friable. Make sure the Land is leveled. Make sure that along the slope, 15-20 ft apart drainage is made.

How to Apply Plant Nutrients

Make sure you apply 8-10 tonnes FYM/ha before land preparation.
Make sure you add 35 kg N, 70 kg P2 O5, and 70 kg K2 O/ha before the last ploughing. If you want to control the termites problem, 350-400 kg Neem Cake / ha can be applied. Try and apply 35-40 kg N as top dressing in September to October. By Para venture if the soil is rich in organic matter, you can reduce N dose.

The Irrigation and Interculture of Aloe Vera plant

Try as much as possible to make sure that after 40 days weeding and earthing up are done. You can also practice earthing up after the top dressing of the fertilizer. One thing about Aloe Vera plant is that they are slightly tolerant to drought, but very sensitive to water stagnation. Which means proper drainage is more important than irrigation.

Chapter four: Pest and disease control in Aloe Vera plant

Aloe Vera plant is like any other plants that also face pest and disease challenge. The following are some of the pest and disease that attack Aloe Vera plant:

1. The Aloe rust:

The symptoms: What you will observe is a small, pale yellow spots on the leaves which can expand and turn brown; The leaves will begin to fall from the plant.

The cause: Fungus

How to manage and control it: This particular disease is self-limiting and it really requires no treatment.

2. The Anthracnose disease:

The symptoms: You will observe the appearance of small round oval, as the disease progress the lesions will join together to form a big necrotic area.

The causes: Fungus

How to manage and control it: Try as much as possible to apply a suitable fungicides.

3. The Basal stem rot Aloe Vera:

The symptoms: What you will observe is the base of the plant turning reddish brown to black and rotting.

The causes: Fungi

How to manage and control it: You can save the pieces of plant by taking cuttings above rotted portion.

4. The Bacterial soft rot of Aloe Vera:

The symptoms: You will observe a watery, rotting leaves which are darker in color. You will see the young leaves wilting and collapsing. Some of the leaves will start bulging due to gas formation inside.

The causes: Bacterium

How to manage and control it: This disease is very fatal. Try as much as possible to avoid over-watering of the Aloe Vera plants.

5. The Aloe vera aphid:

The Symptoms: The insect feed at the bases of the leaves or in rolled ends of damaged leaves. These insects also secrete honeydew. This can lead to slow grow of the Aloe Vera plant.

The causes: Insect

How to manage and control it: Try and apply insecticidal soap.

Chapter five: How to harvest Aloe Vera plant

The Aloe Vera Leaves can be harvested 7-8 months after planting. You can use a sharp knife to harvest. If you want to harvest about 3–4 leaves you can do that by pulling each of the leaf away from the plant stalk. Try as much as possible to handle the leaves gently. A proper care should be taken to avoid damage to the outer rind and to maintain the seal at the base of the leaf in order to avoid the introduction of bacteria. Any of the Leaves that show signs of tip necrosis should not be harvested.

ALOE VERA FARMING

HOW TO START A PROFITABLE ALOE VERA FARM

BY Lucky James

Made in the USA
Monee, IL
20 August 2023

41276256R00016